The Zela Wela Kids

Build a Bank

NANCY PHILLIPS, MBA

AuthorHouse™
1663 Liberty Drive
Bloomington, IN 47403
www.authorhouse.com
Phone: 1-800-839-8640

First published by AuthorHouse 2/11/2010

ISBN: 978-1-4490-7413-5 (sc)

Library of Congress Control Number: 2010900361

Printed in the United States of America
Bloomington, Indiana

This book is printed on acid-free paper.

"This document is sold with the understanding that the author and publisher are not engaged in
rendering legal, accounting, or other professional service. If accounting or legal advice or other expert
assistance is required, the services of a competent professional person should be sought."

authorHOUSE®

To Natasha and Max - my inspiration

The future is yours; believe in your dreams with all your heart and mind. Set your goals and enjoy the steps of your journey, your dreams will unfold before you.

"Hi, Mom!" Jack and Emma called cheerfully.
"Hi, Jack. Hi, Emma. How was school today?"
"Great!" they both replied.

"We got to play outside because it was so nice out," Emma said.
"That's wonderful," said Mom. "I'm glad you had fun. I had a good day, too!"

"Mom, do we have any of those really small cereal boxes at home?" Jack asked
"Yes, I think so, Jack. Why?"

"Mrs. Davies is going to help us build savings banks next week, and we each need four cereal boxes."
"And we need to glue them together this weekend," Emma added.
"That sounds like a fun idea," said Mom. "I think I bought some cereal boxes for camping next weekend. We can look for them when we get home."

"Thanks, Mom," said Emma.

"I'm looking forward to making a savings bank," said Jack excitedly.

"Okay, here are the boxes," said Mom. "Do you know how to glue them together?"

"Yes," replied Emma. "The pictures should be stuck together like this."

"Looks good!" laughed Mom , as she gave Jack and Emma their glue bottles.

"Will you make a slit in each box for us to put the money in, Mom?" asked Jack.
"Sure, Jack. Hand all the boxes to me and I'll do it now before you glue them together."
"Okay, Mom," Jack said happily.
They were both eager to start making their savings banks.

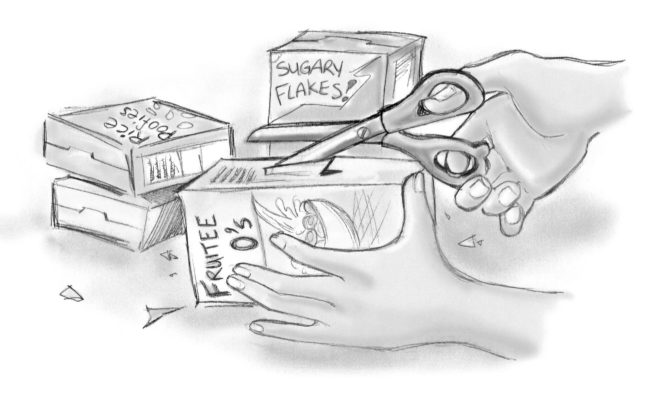

The following Monday, all the children were excited to work on their banks. "Have you all glued your white paper onto the three closed sides of the bank?" asked Mrs. Davies.

"Yes, Mrs. D!" all the students replied. They could hardly wait to find out what they should do next.

"Good. Now let's put names on all the different parts of your banks. On the top box please print the word 'Give.' This is a very important box. This is where you keep the money you will give to people or animals in need of food, shelter or help of some kind. You can also help take care of your planet by giving money to protect our land, water and air here on earth."

"Your parents will help you decide
what charities to give this money to.
I think you will all feel very good inside
when you give to help others. It is one of the
most wonderful things you can do."

"Okay, class. On the second box please print the word 'Invest.' The purpose of putting money in this box is to make your money grow and grow and grow, the same way a little pumpkin seed grows into a big round pumpkin."

"The idea of investing is to use the money you have to make more money, to make it grow. You don't have to start off with a lot of money—quite often just having a great idea can get you on your way. But you need to do it and keep doing it. That's the key. You will learn more about this as you get older. Make sure you ask people lots of questions along the way."

"On the third box please print 'Save.' This box is a place for you to save for things you may want to buy over the next few months, like a toy car or doll."

"Amar, what do you think you would like to save up for?" Mrs. Davies asked.
"I would like to buy my own bike," replied Amar.
"That is an excellent goal, Amar," said Mrs. Davies, smiling.

Mrs. Davies asked the children to label the fourth box with the word "Spend." "The money you put in this box," she explained, "is for little things your parents might allow you to buy during the week, like treats or headbands or trading cards. When you are an adult, this money will also be used to pay for things like food or your telephone bill."

"Mrs. Davies, can we put some pictures of the things we're saving for on our banks?" asked Emma.

"Yes, Emma," answered Mrs. Davies. "That's a wonderful idea. When you have finished putting numbers on the banks, you can draw or paste pictures on them."

"Your parents can help you decide exactly how much money you should put in each box, but for today you will all put the same numbers on your banks. Ask your moms and dads to help you put the money in the correct boxes until you know how to do it by yourselves."

"How do we get the money out of the banks, Mrs. D?" asked Amar.

"Good question, Amar. That's very important! Look at the ends of the boxes where you took out the cereal bags. These will be taped closed before you put your money in. When you want some money from one of your bank boxes, you just peel back the tape and take your money out."

Mrs. Davies asked the children to turn their banks around so they could see the thin side covered with white paper.

"We are going to pretend you all have one dollar to divide up into your four savings bank boxes. On the top box please print '10¢.' This will be the money you give away to help people or animals in need. For every 100¢ or $1 you are given, 10¢ will go in that top box."

"Lucas, what is another way to say '100¢'?"
"One dollar," Lucas answered.
"Very good, Lucas," Mrs. Davies replied.

"Now, on the second box please print '15¢.' This is your investing box. This is the box where you'll save for bigger things like your own land and buildings, a business, or maybe some gold and silver."

"Mrs. D, what is a business?" asked Jack.

"Good question, Jack. A business is made up of people working together to make and sell products or provide a service, like the lady who cuts your mom's hair."

"So if Jack and I open a lemonade stand and sell people drinks, that's a business?" asked Emma.

"Yes, it certainly is, Emma," replied Mrs. D. "The lemonade would be the product you are selling."

"On your third box, print '25¢.' This is where you save for special things you would like to buy. These are bigger, more expensive items that you don't have enough money to buy with your regular spending money. For example, my husband and I are saving for a boat. We plan to buy it next spring."

"For your last box, please print '50¢.' This is your spending money for each week. If you don't spend it all during the week, you can put what's left into your savings box or leave it in the spending box for another time and watch the amount get bigger. When you are finished printing your numbers, you can start decorating your bank with drawings or stickers."

"These look wonderful!" said Mrs. Davies as she walked around looking at everyone's banks. "Don't forget to put your names on them!"

The kids all chattered happily about their new savings banks.

"Mom, look at our banks!" Emma exclaimed.

"They are fantastic, you two!" Mom exclaimed. "I love the bright colors. And look at your printing! Nice work! Do you want to put your money in them when you get home?"

"Sure!" said Jack.

"Yes, I do!" agreed Emma.

"Okay, you two, let's put your money in the banks. Where should we start?"

"At the top, Mom," replied Emma.

"Sure, Emma. That's a good place to start. So, what coin is equal to 10¢?"

"A dime," Emma said, smiling and holding up a dime.

"Excellent!" said Mom. "Go ahead and put a dime in your Giving box."

"What do you think you would like to do with your giving money when the box is full Jack?" asked Mom.

"I want to help the puppies that don't have a home, like the one we saw running by the road," said Jack.

"That's a really great idea, Jack. How about you, Emma?"

"I would like to send it to Africa to help those kids we sent the Christmas presents to. They don't have food or clean water so they really need the money," said Emma thoughtfully. "I'm so glad we can help them."

"Yes, Emma. I am glad, too, and very proud that you are helping," said Mom as she put her arm around each of them.

"For your second box, the investing part, it looks like you want 15¢. To make 15¢ you need a dime and a nickel, or you could use pennies. Do you both have a dime and a nickel?"

"Yes, Mom," the twins replied.

"Good. And what is investing for?" asked Mom.

"To make our money grow so when we're older we can do lots of fun things," replied Jack.

"Right, Jack. Having money that's well invested gives you choices about what you can do, which is definitely lots of fun!"

"Okay, the third box is your 'Saving' box. How much are you going to put in it?"
"25¢, a quarter," Emma said, dropping in a quarter. Jack put his quarter in as well.
"What are you two saving for?" asked Mom.
"Roller skates!" Emma exclaimed.
"A Blueback racetrack," replied Jack.
"Great ideas, you two," said Mom, smiling.

"Now let's go to the last box, the spending box," said Mom. "You get to put in 50¢. What makes 50¢?"
"Two quarters, the biggest silver coins," answered Jack.
"That's correct, Jack. Each quarter is worth 25¢, so you need two of them. Go ahead and put two quarters in your last box. And what's this money for?"
For when we want treats or little things at the store," answered Emma.
"Exactly," said Mom. "And it's up to you to manage your spending money wisely.

You have now split up your 100¢ into four different savings boxes. Well done! Mrs. Davies' idea is really great. I think I'll do the same thing!"

"Ah, Mom, you're being silly," teased Jack.
"Not really, Jack. This is a fantastic way for adults to manage their money, too. The boxes may just need to be bigger. Now, I think your hard work deserves a treat. Who's ready for something yummy to eat?"
"We are!" the twins cheered.

LaVergne, TN USA
20 May 2010
183243LV00002B